GERANIUM.

XERANTHEMUM.

THIS CATALOGUE IS OUR ONLY SALESMAN.

THANKS GIVING PRUNE

RED CROSS CURRANT

NIAGARA PEACH LARGEST AND BEST OF ALL

BANANA APPLE

FANNY APPLE

GREEN'S NURSERY CO.
ROCHESTER, N.Y.
FRUIT GUIDE AND CATALOGUE FOR THE YEAR 1904

At Home in the Garden
The Musings of a Victorian Gardener

Gail Hamilton, 1862

Edited by Pat Ross

CHRONICLE BOOKS
SAN FRANCISCO

PRINTED IN SINGAPORE.

BOOK AND COVER DESIGN: JILL JACOBSON.

LIBRARY OF CONGRESS
CATALOGING-IN-PUBLICATION
DATA AVAILABLE.

ISBN: 0-8118-0733-9

DISTRIBUTED IN CANADA BY
RAINCOAST BOOKS, 8680 CAMBIE STREET,
VANCOUVER, B.C. V6P 6M9

10 9 8 7 6 5 4 3 2 1

CHRONICLE BOOKS • 275 FIFTH STREET
SAN FRANCISCO, CALIFORNIA 94103

I cannot resist the dustiest old books at a tag sale, the somber shelves of an antiquarian bookshop, or a bustling ephemera show where rare books share space with antique paper collectibles. The ephemera shows that advertise themselves as "paper extravaganzas" always sound more enticing somehow, promising a carnival mood rather than a hall of scholarly book dealers.

It seems appropriate that an "extravaganza" is where I came upon Gail Hamilton's 1862 volume, *Country Living and Country Thinking*. My dowdy edition could hardly be considered rare or beautiful. It lacks an elegant leather binding embossed with gold or hand tooling, the page design is rather plain, and the type is cramped and faded. The front cover has now pulled away entirely from the spine, and it will cost more to repair properly than the book cost me in the first place. But standing in a crowded booth, I was attracted first by the title and then by the author's spirited voice. A paragraph or two was enough to convince me that Gail Hamilton was a woman who did not suffer fools gladly, and her book of essays would be a sound investment.

The New York subway would not seem the most fitting place to curl up with a hundred-year-old-plus book, but I was late and in a hurry for something to read, and *Country Living and Country Thinking* happened to be located on the table closest to the door. Given the erratic schedules of the New York Transit System, I had ample time to discover the wit and opinionated charm of this author before I reached my stop. Her interests and knowledge ran the gamut—offering up a regular minestrone of topics—from the war between the sexes and her deep affection for a friend's child, to patriotism and slavery. Without catching her breath and never allowing readers to catch theirs, Gail Hamilton moved from one topic to the next with unbridled enthusiasm and a breakneck speed. But it was her essays on gardening that slowed me to a leisurely pace as I savored the author's heartfelt advice. Lurching downtown on the Lexington Avenue local, I actually found myself laughing out loud, and alone—more the behavior of underground lunatics and desperados.

An 1873 *New York Tribune* summed up the writing of Gail Hamilton in a review of her style: "Gail Hamilton exhibits a singular intellectual versatility, nimbly bounding from an exuberant and almost rollicking play of humor to the most serious and impressive appeals." Born Mary Abigail Dodge in 1833, the writer who used the pseudonym Gail Hamilton knew at the age of twenty-two that a writing career was her calling. "I want an end and aim in life, and see no other way to obtain it," she wrote in a covering letter to the editor of the *National Era*, an antislavery publication where *Uncle Tom's Cabin* first appeared. She went on: "I do not ask for charity, nor for a friendly judgment, but for a just one. If you think the pieces worthless, you will not hesitate to say so and I promise not to drown myself thereupon." The editor accepted the pieces immediately, replying: ". . . Your pen is not a commonplace one," and ". . . you *do* write a little masculinely."

Mary Abigail Dodge took "Hamilton" from her birthplace and

home in Hamilton, Massachusetts. She apparently liked the gender ambiguity of the "Gail" in Abigail. It is perhaps too easy to surmise that she felt more comfortable pursuing her vigorous and rationalistic style as the androgynous Gail, though at times she declares openly that she is a woman. Her real-life nickname was Abby, though she often signed her letters M.A.D. In *Gail Hamilton's Life in Letters*, the author writes passionately of her desire to maintain a private life apart from her writing, guarding her true identity throughout a writing career that produced nearly a dozen books and a sizeable number of articles. Mary Abigail Dodge led a life of privilege—well educated, well read, well travelled—and preferred to keep her professional talents known only to a close group of friends, among them John Greenleaf Whittier.

It is not surprising that Gail Hamilton shared a special feeling for the writings of Whittier and Henry David Thoreau, and for their love of nature. Throughout her essays, she writes eloquently of the seasons and of growing things. Living in rural Massachusetts in the mid-1800s, her life was that of a country girl. She frequently speaks of days on a farm. Nature did, however, get the best of her in *Country Living and Country Thinking*, prompting Hamilton to approach the subject of her vegetable and flower garden with an effervescent wit equal to the task. Perhaps the only arena where Hamilton backed down, or at least backed off, was in nature, where she knew who had the upper hand. But her energy and her determination were rarely daunted.

The authenticity of the events in Gail Hamilton's essays on gardening is a puzzlement. Her writing would indicate that she and a male companion, nicknamed (by her) Halicarnassus, shared a country home on Long Island Sound, during which time a vegetable garden failed and a flower garden rewarded her in abundance the following spring. Yet her personal letters as published in

Gail Hamilton's Life in Letters do not bear this out. Also puzzling is the author's relationship with Halicarnassus, her helpmate as well as her constant mental sparring partner. Perhaps Hamilton was having fun at the expense of her male companion by making erudite references to ancient history and geography. After all, the city of Helicarnassus is the birthplace of the historians Herodotus and Dionysius. Or perhaps this was a reference to the athlete, Helicarnassian Agaiscles, who, upon winning in the ancient games, defied the laws by carrying home the trophy. At any rate, the husbandlike figure of Halicarnassus in Hamilton's story remains a mystery. The author never married; in fact, on the subject of marriage, she had strong opinions: "I suppose the husband-and-child idea is the natural one, but we have so mistaken the letter for the spirit, and so crushed with the letter, that sometimes I feel rather disgusted with the whole thing. . . ."

Since Gail Hamilton's imagination ran larger than life, it is conceivable that Halicarnassus was of the author's vivid imagination, inspired perhaps by her longtime friendship with S.S. Wood, her coeditor of a popular household magazine. Hamilton's correspondence with Mr. Wood reveals the same smug intellectual standoffs, the same bickering over issues both trivial and monumental, the same unmovable attitudes when emotional storms brewed; then, ultimately, an abiding affection and unwavering support. There is everything to indicate that the author played with the notion of her Halicarnassus the same way she played with her readers, leading them through the vivid leaps of her mind—from joy to despair in the very same breath. Her essays are richly embroidered tapestries in which Hamilton appears to commune in her mind with figures real and fan-tastical, combining the two at whim. The readers' ultimate lessons were to be gleaned from the principles of the author; how the author achieved her end was fair game.

If there is fault to find with Gail Hamilton, then it is with her breathless sentences and her delight with punctuation; also with an overzealous style that occasionally indulges itself pages beyond its point. In gathering together the best of her thoughts on gardening, I used a gentle pen to sift her words, sort her thoughts, and cull the most salient reflections, taking care to respect the original intentions of the writer. I am, after all, a writer, too—and a writer who was once an editor. I have known both sides of that blue pencil. But, I have reasoned that it is better to know Gail Hamilton with fewer commas, dashes, and semicolons than never to know Gail Hamilton at all.

My own gardening efforts are fraught with peril. My delicate skin has only to feel a breeze of poison ivy fumes in the wind, and I begin to itch. Dressed for a wilderness adventure, I venture into my garden. Perhaps this is why I appreciate the fruits of anyone's labors, and empathize with both Gail Hamilton's heartbreaks and victories where vegetables and flowers are concerned. As a child, I used to check my carrot seeds in the middle of the night—lonely specks beneath the dark soil of some childhood project. One of my favorite books remains *The Carrot Seed*. I know, as the child in the book knows, that the carrot will come up. Our lives are, after all, a pushing through the soil of that spirited seed, overcoming the elements to bloom at last. Gail Hamilton writes about more than gardening in *At Home in the Garden*; she writes about eternal hope. I believe that she and I would have been friends if our paths had crossed.

PAT ROSS

can speak of it calmly now; but there have been moments when
the lightest mention of those words would sway my soul to its profoundest depths.
I am a woman. You may have inferred this before; but I now desire to state it
distinctly, because I like to do as I would be done by, when I can just as well
as not. It rasps a person of my temperament exceedingly to be deceived.

When anyone tells a story, we wish to know at the outset whether the story-teller is a man or a woman. The two sexes awaken two entirely distinct sets of feelings, and you would no more use the one for the other than you would put out your tiny teacups at breakfast, or lay the carving knife by the butter plate. Consequently it is very exasperating to sit, open-eyed and expectant, watching the removal of the successive swathings which hide from you the dusky glories of an old-time princess, and, when the unrolling is over, to find it is nothing, after all, but a great lubberly boy. Equally trying is it to feel your interest clustering round a narrator's manhood, all your individuality merging in his, till, of a sudden, by the merest chance, you catch the swell of crinoline, and there you are. Away with such clumsiness! Let us have everybody christened before we begin.

I do, therefore, with Spartan firmness, depose and say that I am a woman. I am aware that I place myself at signal disadvantage by the avowal. I fly in the face of hereditary prejudice. I am thrust at once beyond the pale of masculine sympathy. Men will neither credit my success nor lament my failure, because they will consider me poaching on their manor. If I chronicle a big beet, they will bring forward one twice as large. If I mourn a deceased squash, they will mutter, "Woman's farming!"

I could easily deceive you, if I chose. There is about my serious style a vigor of thought, a comprehensiveness of view, a closeness of logic, and a terseness of diction, com-monly supposed to pertain only to the stronger sex. Not wanting in a certain fanciful spright-liness which is the peculiar grace of woman, it possesses also, in large measure, that concentra-tiveness which is deemed the peculiar strength of man. Where an ordinary woman will leave

13

the beaten track, wandering in a thousand little byways of her own flowery and beautiful, it is true, and leading her airy feet to "sunny spots of greenery" and the gleam of golden apples, but keeping her not less surely from the goal, I march straight on, turning neither to the right hand nor to the left, beguiled into no side issues, discussing no collateral question, but with

keen eye and strong hand aiming right at the heart of my theme.

You will, therefore, no longer withhold your appreciative admiration, when, in full possession of what theologians call the power of contrary choice, I make the unmistakable assertion that I am a woman.

*H*ope told a flattering tale when, excited and happy, but not sated with the gayeties of a sojourn among urban and urbane friends, I set out on my triumphal march from the city of my visit to the estate of my adoption. Triumphal indeed! My pathway was strewed with roses. Feathery asparagus and the crispness of tender lettuce waved dewy greetings from every railroad side; green peas crested the racing waves of Long Island Sound, and unnumbered carrots of gold sprang up in the wake of the ploughing steamer; till I was well-nigh drunk with the new wine of my own purple vintage. But I was not ungenerous.

15

In the height of my innocent exultation, I remembered the dwellers in cities who do all their gardening at stalls, and in my heart I determined, when the season should be fully blown, to invite as many as my house could hold to share with me the delight of plucking strawberries from their stems and drinking in foaming health from the balmy-breathed cows. Moreover, in the exuberance of my joy, I determined to go still further, and despatch to those doomed ones who cannot purchase even a furlough from burning pavements baskets of fragrance and sweetness. I pleased myself with pretty conceits.

To one who toils early and late in an official Sahara, that

perfume, I would send a bunch of long-stemmed white and

dainty note whispering, "Dear Fritz: drink this pure glass

not forgetting your unforgetful friend." To a pale-browed,

dered flounces to the bedside of an invalid mother whom

devotion can scarcely keep this side the pearly gates, I woul

cool, green leaves into their straitened home, and with eyes

Maria, the peaches are to go to your lips, the bloom to your

much grace and gladness may bud and blossom in one little

surprises, unexpected tenderness, grateful joys, hopes, loves

sparkles of mirth, what sweeps of summer in the heart,

the home atmosphere may always be redolent of

rimson rosebuds, in the midst of which he should find a

f my overflowing June to the health of weans and wife,

ad-eyed woman, who flits from velvet carpets and broi-

er slender fingers and unslender and most godlike

eap a basket of summer-hued peaches smiling up from

erchance, tear-dimmed, she should read, "My good

heeks, and the gardener to your heart." Ah me! How

arden! Only three acres of land, but what a crop of sunny

nd restful memories!—what wells of happiness, what

vhat glimpses of the Upper Country!

17

I SAY – THE MURPHYS are a noted family – among them
NEW EARLY SUNRISE
Has proved itself the earliest of all, producing potatoes fit for
the table in fifty two days from time of planting.
(2) largest potatoes in a crop grown from one (1)pound in
sixty-seven (67)days weighed twenty-five (25) pounds

Halicarnassus was there before me in the garden. It has been the one misfortune of my life that Halicarnassus got the start of me at the outset. With a fair field and no favor I should have been quite adequate to him. As it was, he was born and began, and there was no resource left to me but to be born and follow, which I did as fast as possible; but that one false move could never be redeemed.

If mind could have been supreme over matter, Halicarnassus should, in the first place, have taken the world at second hand from me, and, in the second place, he should not have stood smiling on the front-door steps when the coach set me down there. As it was, I made the best of the one case by following in his footsteps, not meekly, not acquiescently, but protesting, yet following and of the other, by smiling responsive and asking pleasantly—

"Are the things planted yet?"

"No," said Halicarnassus.

This was better than I had dared to hope. When I saw him standing there so complacent and serene, I felt certain that a storm was brewing, or rather had brewed, and burst over my garden, and blighted its fair prospects. I was confident that he had gone and planted every square inch of the soil with some hideous absurdity, which would spring up a hundred-fold in perpetual reminders of the one misfortune to which I have alluded.

So his ready answer gave me relief, and yet I could not divest myself of a vague fear, a sense of coming thunder. In spite of my endeavors, that calm, clear face would lift itself to my view as a mere "weather-breeder"; but I ate my supper, unpacked my trunks, took out my papers of precious seeds, and, sitting in the flooding sunlight under the little western porch, I poured them into my lap, and bade Halicarnassus come to me. He came, I am sorry to say, with a pipe in his mouth.

"Do you wish to see my jewels?" I asked, looking as much like Cornelia as a little woman somewhat inclined to dumpiness can.

Halicarnassus nodded assent.

19

20

21

22

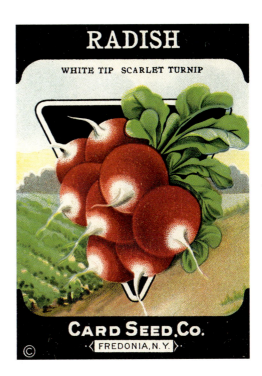

"There," said I, unrolling a paper, "that is LYCHNIDEA ACUMINATA. Sometimes it flowers in white masses, pure as a baby's soul. Sometimes it glows in purple, pink, and crimson, intense, but unconsuming, like Horeb's burning bush. The old Greeks knew it well, and they baptized its prismatic loveliness with their sunny symbolism, and called it the Flame-Flower. These very seeds may have sprung centuries ago from the hearts of heroes who sleep at Marathon; and when their tender petals quiver in the sunlight of my garden, I shall see the gleam of Attic armor and the flash of royal souls. Like heroes, too, it is both beautiful and bold. It does not demand careful cultivation —no hot-house tenderness."

"I should rather think not," interrupted Halicarnassus. "Pat Curran has his front yard full of it."

I collapsed at once, and asked, humbly, "Where did he get it?"

"Got it anywhere. It grows wild almost. It's nothing but phlox. My opinion is that the old Greeks knew no more about it than that brindled cow."

Nothing further occurring to me to be said on the subject, I waived it, and took up another parcel, on which I spelled out, with some difficulty,

"DELPHINIUM EXALTATUM. Its name indicates its nature."

**"It's an exalted dolphin, then, I suppose,"
said Halicarnassus.**

"*Yes!*" I said, dexterously catching up an ARGUMENTUM AD HOMINEM, it is an exalted dolphin, an apotheosized dolphin, a dolphin made glorious. For, as the dolphin catches the sunbeams and sends them back with a thousand added splendors, so this flower opens its quivering bosom and gathers from the vast laboratory of the sky the purple of a monarch's robe and the ocean's deep, calm blue. In its gracious cup you shall see."

25

**"A fiddlestick!" jerked out Halicarnassus, profanely.
"What are you raving about such a precious bundle
of weeds for? There isn't a shoemaker's apprentice
in the village that has his seven-by-nine garden
overrun with them. You might have done better
than bring cartloads of phlox and larkspur a
thousand miles. Why didn't you import a few
hollyhocks, or a sunflower or two, and perhaps
a dainty slip of cabbage? A pumpkin vine, now,
would climb over the front door deliciously,
and a row of burdocks would make
a highly entertaining border."**

The reader will bear me witness that I had met my first rebuff with humility. It was probably this very humility that emboldened him to a second attack. I determined to change my tactics and give battle.

"Halicarnassus," said I, severely, "you are a hypocrite. You set up for a Democrat."

"Not I," interrupted he. "I voted for Harrison in '40, and for Fremont in the '50s, and . . . ."

"Nonsense!" interrupted I, in turn. "I mean a Democrat etymological, not a Democrat political. You stand by the Declaration of Independence, and believe in liberty, equality, and fraternity, and that all men are of one blood; and here you are, ridiculing these innocent flowers, because their brilliant beauty is not shut up in a conservatory, to exhale its fragrance on a fastidious few, but blooms on all alike, gladdening the home of exile and lightening the burden of labor."

Halicarnassus saw that I had made a point against him, and preserved a discreet silence.

"But you are wrong," I went on, "even if you are right. You may laugh to scorn my floral treasures, because they seem to you common and unclean, but your laughter is premature. It is no ordinary seed that you see before you. It sprang from no profane soil. It came from some kind of an office at Washington sir! It was given me by one whose name stands high on the scroll of fame—a statesman whose views are as broad as his judgment is sound, an orator who holds all hearts in his hand, a man who is always found on the side of the feeble truth against the strong falsehoods, whose sympathy for all that is good, whose hostility to all that is bad, and whose boldness in every righteous cause make him alike the terror and abhorrence of the oppressed, and the hope and joy and staff of the oppressed."

**"What is his name?"
said Halicarnassus, phlegmatically.**

27

"And for your miserable pumpkin vine," I went on, "behold this morning glory, that shall open its barbaric splendor to the sun and mount heaven-ward on the sparkling chariots of the dew. I took this from the white hand of a young girl in whose heart poetry and purity have met, grace and virtue have kissed each other, whose feet have danced over lilies and roses, who has known no sterner

duty than to give caresses, and whose gentle, spontaneous, and ever-active loveliness continually remind me that of such is the kingdom of heaven."

**"Courted yet?" asked Halicarnassus,
with a show of interest.**

MOON FLOWER
PRICE
10¢

HUTH SEED CO.
SAN ANTONIO, TEXAS

I transfixed him with a look, and continued—

"This MAURANDIA, a climber, it may
be common or it may be a king's ransom. I only know
that it is rosy-hued, and that I shall look at life through
its pleasant medium. Some fantastic trellis, brown and benevolent, shall knot supporting arms around it, and day by day it
shall twine daintily toward my southern window and whisper
softly of the sweet-voiced, tender-eyed woman from whose fairy
bower it came in rosy wrappings. And this NEMOPHILA, 'blue as
my brother's eyes,' the brave young brother whose heroism and
manhood have outstripped his years, and who looks forth from
the dark leafiness of far Australia lovingly and longingly over the
blue waters, as if, floating above them, he might catch the flutter
of white garments and the smile on a sister's lip—"

"What are you going to do with 'em?"
put in Halicarnassus again.

I hesitated a moment, undecided whether to be amiable or bel-
licose under the provocation, but concluded that my ends would stand
a better chance of being gained by adopting the former course, and so
answered seriously, as if I had not been switched off the track, but was
going on with perfect continuity—

"Tomorrow I shall take observations. Then, where the situation seems most favorable, I shall lay out a garden. I shall plant these seeds in it, except the vines and such things, which I wish to put near the house to hide as much as possible its garish white. Then, with every little tender shoot that appears above the ground, there will blossom also a pleasant memory, or a sunny hope, or an admiring thrill."

"What do you expect will be the market value of that crop?"

"Wealth which an empire could not purchase," I answered, with enthusiasm. "But I shall not confine my attention to flowers. I shall make the useful go with the beautiful. I shall plant vegetables, lettuce, and asparagus, and so forth. Our table shall be garnished with the products of our own soil, and our own works shall praise us."

29

There was a pause of several minutes, during which I fondled the seeds, and Halicarnassus enveloped himself in clouds of smoke. Presently there was a cessation of puffs. A rift in the cloud showed that the oracle was opening his mouth, and directly thereafter he delivered himself of the encouraging remark.

"If we don't have any vegetables till we raise 'em, we shall be carnivorous for some time to come."

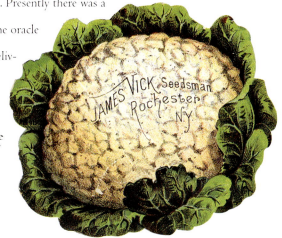

*T*t was said with that provoking indifference more trying to a sensitive mind than downright insult. You know it is based on some hidden obstacle, palpable to your enemy, though hidden from you, and that he is calm because he knows that the nature of things will work against you, so that he need not interfere. If I had been less interested, I would have revenged myself on him by remaining silent; but I was very much interested, so I strangled my pride and said, "Why not?"

"Land is too old for such things. Soil isn't mellow enough."

I had always supposed that the greater part of the mainland of our continent was of equal antiquity, and dated back alike to the alluvial period; but I suppose our little three acres must have been injected through the intervening strata by some physical convulsion from the drift, or the tertiary formation, perhaps even from the primitive granite.

"What are you going to do?" I ventured to inquire. "I don't suppose the land will grow any younger by keeping."

"Plant it with corn and potatoes for at least two years before there can be anything like a garden."

And Halicarnassus put up his pipe and betook himself to the house—and I was glad of it, the abominable bore! to sit there and listen to my glowing schemes, knowing all the while that they were soap bubbles. "Corn and potatoes," indeed! I didn't believe a word of it. Halicarnassus always had an insane passion for corn and potatoes. Land represented to him so many bushels of the one or the other. Now corn and potatoes are very well in their way, but, like every other innocent indulgence carried too far, become a vice; and I more than suspected he had planned the strategy simply to gratify his own weakness. Corn and potatoes, indeed!

But when Halicarnassus entered the lists against me, he found an opponent worthy of his steel. A few more such victories would be his ruin. A grand scheme fired and filled my mind during the silent watches of the night, and sent me forth in the morning, jubilant with high resolve. Alexander might weep that he had no more worlds to conquer; but I would create new. Archimedes might desiderate a place to stand on, before he could bring his lever into play; I would move the world, self-poised. If Halicarnassus fancied that I was cut up, dispersed, and annihilated by one disaster, he should weep tears of blood to see me rise, phoenixlike, from the ashes of my dead hopes, to a newer and more glorious life. Here, having exhausted my classics, I took a long sweep down to modern times, and vowed in my heart never to give up the ship.

*H*alicarnassus saw that a fell purpose was working in my mind, but a certain high tragedy in my aspect warned him to silence; so he only dogged me around the corners of the house, eyed me askance from the woodshed, and peeped through the crevices of the demented little barn. But his vigilance bore no fruit. I but walked moodily with folded arms and fixed eyes, or struck out new paths at random, so long as there were any vestiges of his creation extant. His time and patience being at length exhausted, he went into the field to immolate himself with ever new devotion on the shrine of corn and potatoes. Then my scheme came to a head at once. In my walking, I had observed a box about three feet long, two broad, and one foot deep, which Halicarnassus, with his usual disregard of the proprieties of life, had used to block up a gateway that was waiting for a gate. It was just what I wanted.

I straightaway knocked out the few nails that kept it in place, and, like another Samson, bore it away on my shoulders. It was not an easy thing to manage, as anyone may find by trying—nor would I advise young ladies, as a general thing, to adopt that form of exercise—but the end, not the means, was my object, and by skillful diplomacy I got it up the back stairs and through my window, out upon the roof of the porch directly below. I then took the ash pail and the fire shovel, and went into the field, carefully keeping the lee-side of Halicarnassus.

"GOOD, RICH LOAM," I had observed all the gardening books to recommend; but wherein the virtue or the richness of loam con-

sisted I did not feel competent to decide, and I scorned to ask.

There seemed to be two kinds: one black, damp, and dismal; the

other fine, yellow, and good-natured. A little reflection decided

me to take the latter. Gold constituted riches, and this was yel-

low like gold. Moreover, it seemed to have more life in it. Night

and darkness belonged to the other, while the very heart of sun-

shine and summer seemed to be imprisoned in this golden dust.

So I plied my shovel and filled my pail again and again, bearing

it aloft with joyful labor, eager to be through before Halicarnassus should reappear; but

he got on the trail just as I was whisking upstairs for the last time, and shouted, astonished—

"What are you doing?"

"Nothing," I answered, with that well-known accent which says,

"Everything! and I mean to keep doing it."

I have observed, that, in managing parents, husbands, lovers, brothers, and

indeed all classes of inferiors, nothing is so efficacious as to let them know at the outset that

you are going to have your own way. They may fret a little at first, and interpose a few puny

obstacles, but it will be only a temporary obstruction; whereas, if you parley and hesitate and

suggest, they will but gather courage and strength for a formidable resistance. It is the first

step that costs. Halicarnassus understood at once from my one small shot that I was in a

mood to be let alone, and he let me alone accordingly.

I remembered he had said that the soil was not mellow enough, and I determined that my soil should be mellow, to which end I took it up by handfuls and squeezed it through my fingers, completely pulverizing it. It was not disagreeable work. Things in their right places are very seldom disagreeable. A spider on your dress is a horror, but a spider outdoors is rather interesting. Besides, the loam had a fine, soft feel that was absolutely pleasant; but a hideous black-and-yellow reptile with horns and hoofs, that winked up at me from it, was decidedly unpleasant and out of place, and I at once concluded that the soil was sufficiently mellow for my purposes, and smoothed it off directly. Then, with delighted fingers, in

sweeping circles and fantastic whirls and exact triangles

I planted my seeds in generous profusion, determined that, if my wilderness did not blossom, it should not be from niggardliness of seed. But even then my box was full before my basket was emptied, and I was very reluctantly compelled to bring down from the garret another box, which had been the property of my great-grandfather.

My great-grandfather was, I regret to say, a barber. I would rather never have had any. If there is anything in the world besides worth that I reverence, it is ancestry. My whole life long have I been in search of a pedigree, and though I run well at the beginning, I invariably stop short at the third remove by running my head into a barber's shop. If he had only been a farmer; now, I should not have minded. There is something dignified and antique in land, and no one need trouble himself to ascertain whether "farmer" stood for a close-fisted, narrow-souled clodhopper, or the smiling, benevolent master of broad acres.

I must say, with all deference to my great-grandfather, that I do wish he would have been considerate enough of his descendants' feelings to have been born in the old days when barbers and doctors were one, or else have chosen some other occupation than barbering. Barber he did, however; in this very box he kept his wigs, and, painful as it was to have continually before my eyes this perpetual reminder of plebeian great-grand-paternity, I consented to it rather than lose my seeds. Then I folded my hands in sweet, though calm satisfaction. I had proved myself equal to the emergency, and that always diffuses a glow of genial complacency through the soul. I had outwitted Halicarnassus. Exultation number two. He had designed to cheat me out of my garden by a story about land, and here was my garden ready to burst forth into blossom under my eyes. He said little, but I knew he felt deeply. I caught him one day looking out at my window with corroding envy in every lineament.

35

**"You might have got some dust out of the road;
it would have been nearer."**

That was all he said. Even that little I did not fully understand.

*T*watched, and waited, and watered, in silent expectancy, for several days, but nothing came up, and I began to be anxious. Suddenly I thought of my vegetable seeds, and determined to try those. Of course a hanging kitchen garden was not to be thought of, and as Halicarnassus was fortunately absent for a few days, I prospected on the farm. A sunny little corner on a southern slope smiled up at me, and seemed to offer itself as a delightful situation for the diminutive garden which mine must be. The soil, too, seemed as fine and mellow as could be desired. I at once captured an Englishman from a neighboring plantation, hurried him into my corner, and bade him dig me and hoe me and plant me a garden as soon as possible. He looked blankly at me for a moment, and I looked blankly at him, wondering what lion he saw in the way.

"Them is planted with potatoes now,"
he gasped, at length.

"No matter," I returned, with sudden relief to find that nothing but potatoes interfered. "I want it to be unplanted, and planted with vegetables—lettuce and asparagus and such."

He stood hesitating.
"Will the master like it?"

"Yes," said Diplomacy, "he will be delighted."
"No matter whether he likes it or not,"
codiciled Conscience. *"You do it."*

"I don't exactly like to take the responsibility," wavered this modern Faint-Heart.

"I don't want you to take the responsibility," I ejaculated, with volcanic vehemence. "I'll take the responsibility. You take the hoe!"

37

PARKER & WOOD,
SEEDS AND TOOLS,
49 North Market St.
BOSTON.
over

Clay & Richmond, Buffalo, N.Y.

These duty people do infuriate me. They are so afraid to do anything that isn't laid out in a right-angled triangle. Every path must be graded and turfed before they dare set their scrupulous feet in it. I like conscience, but, like corn and potatoes, carried too far, it becomes a vice. I think I could commit a murder with less hesitation than some people buy a ninepenny calico. And to see that man stand here, balancing probabilities over a piece of ground no bigger than a bed quilt, as if a nation's fate were at stake, was enough to ruffle a calmer temper than mine. My impetuosity impressed him, however, and he began to lay about him vigorously with hoe and rake and lines, and, in an incredibly short space of time, had a bit of figure flatness laid out with wonderful precision.

38

Meanwhile I had ransacked my vegetable bag, and, though lettuce and asparagus were not there, plenty of beets and parsnips and squashes, etc., were. I let him take his choice. He took the first two. The rest were left on my hands. But I had gone too far to recede. They burned in my pocket for a few days, and I saw that I must get them into the ground somewhere. I could not sleep with them in the room. They were wandering shades, craving at my hands a burial, and I determined to put them where Banquo's ghost would not go—down. Down accordingly they went, but not symmetrically nor simultaneously.

I faced Halicarnassus on the subject of the beet bed, and though I cannot say that either of us gained a brilliant victory, yet I can say that I kept possession of the ground; still, I did not care to risk a second encounter. So I kept my seeds about me continually, and dropped them surreptitiously as occasion offered. Consequently, my garden, taken as a whole, was located where the Penobscot Indian was born—"all along shore." The squashes were scattered among the corn. The beans were tucked under the brushwood, in the fond hope that they would climb up it. Two tomato plants were lodged in the potato field, under the protection of some broken apple branches dragged thither for the purpose. The cucumbers went down on the sheltered side of a woodpile. The peas took their chances of life under the sink-nose. The sweet corn was marked off from the rest by a broomstick and all took root alike in my heart.

39

May I ask you now, O friend, who, I would fain believe, have followed me thus far with no hostile eyes, to glide in tranced forgetfulness through the white blooms of May and the roses of June, into the warm breath of July afternoons and the languid pulse of August, perhaps even into the mild haze of September and the "flying gold" of brown October?

In narrating to you the fruition of my hopes, I shall endeavor to preserve that calm equanimity which is the birthright of royal minds. I shall endeavor not to be unduly elated by success nor unduly depressed by failure, but to state in simple language the result of my experiments, both for an encouragement and a warning. I shall give the history of the several ventures separately, as nearly as I can recollect in the order in which they grew, beginning with the humbler ministers to our appetites, and soaring gradually into the region of the poetical and the beautiful.

he beets came up, little red-veined leaves, struggling for breath among a tangle of Roman wormwood and garlic; and though they exhibited great tenacity of life, they also exhibited great irregularity of purpose. In one spot there would be nothing, in an adjacent spot a whorl of beets, big and little, crowding and jostling and elbowing each other, like schoolboys round the red-hot stove on a winter's morning. I knew they had been planted in a right line, and I don't even now comprehend why they should not come up in a right line. I weeded them, and though freedom from foreign growth discovered an intention of straightness, the most casual observer could not but see that skewness had usurped its place. I repaired to my friend the gardener. He said they must be thinned out and transplanted. It went to my heart to pull up the dear things, but I did it, and set them down again tenderly in the vacant spots. It was evening.

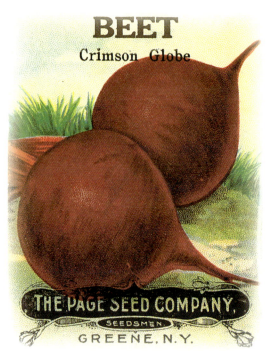

BEET
Crimson Globe

THE PAGE SEED COMPANY,
SEEDSMEN
GREENE, N.Y.

The next morning I went to them. Flatness has a new meaning to me since that morning. You can hardly conceive that anything could look so utterly forlorn, disconsolate, disheartened, and collapsed. In fact, they exhibited a degree of depression so entirely beyond what the circumstances demanded, that I was enraged. If they had shown any symptoms of trying to live, I could have sighed and forgiven them; but, on the contrary, they had flopped and died without a struggle, and I pulled them up without a pang, comforting myself with the remaining ones, which throve on their companions' graves, and waxed fat and full and crimson-hearted, in their soft, brown beds. So delighted was I with their luxuriant rotundity, that I made an internal resolve that henceforth I would always plant beets. True, I cannot abide beets. Their fragrance and their flavor are alike nauseating; but they come up, and a beet that will come up is better than a cedar of Lebanon that won't. In all the vegetable kingdom I know of no quality better than this growth, nor any quality that will atone for its absence.

43

They ran the race with an indescribable vehemence that fairly threw the beets into the shade. They trod so delicately at first that I was quite unprepared for such enthusiasm. Lacking the red veining, I could not distinguish them from the weeds with any certainty, and was forced to let both grow together till the harvest. So both grew together, a perfect jungle. But the parsnips got ahead, and rushed up gloriously, magnificently, bacchanalian as the winds come when forests are rended, as the waves come when navies are stranded. I am, indeed, troubled with a suspicion that their vitality has all run to leaves, and that, when I go down into the depths of the earth for the parsnips I shall find only bread of emptiness. It is a pleasing reflection that parsnips cannot be eaten till the second year. I am told that they must lie in the ground during the winter. Consequently it cannot be decided whether there are any or not till next spring. I shall in the meantime assume and assert, without hesitation or qualification, that there are as many tubers below the surface as there are leaves above it. I shall thereby enjoy a pleasant consciousness, and the respect of all, for the winter; and if disappointment awaits me in the spring, time will have blunted its keenness for me, and other people will have forgotten the whole subject. You may be sure I shall not remind them of it.

Clay & Richmond, Buffalo, N.Y.

A word to the wise is sufficient
USE THE BAY STATE FERTILIZER,
MANUFACTURED BY
THE CLARK'S COVE GUANO COMPANY,
NEW BEDFORD, MASS.
(over)

he cucumbers came up so far, and stuck. It must have been innate depravity, for there was no shadow of reason why they should not keep on as they began. They did not. They stopped growing in the prime of life. Only three cucumbers developed, and they hid under the vines so that I did not see them till they had become ripe, yellow, soft, and worthless. They are an unwholesome fruit at best, and I bore their loss with great fortitude.

47

oth dead. I had been instructed to protect them from the frost by night and from the sun by day. I intended to do so ultimately, but I did not suppose there was any emergency. A frost came the first night and killed them, and a hot sun the next day burned up all there was left. When they were both thoroughly dead, I took great pains to cover them every night and noon. No symptoms of revival appeared to reward my efforts. I left them to shift for themselves. I do not think there was any need of their dying in the first place; and if they would be so absurd as to die without provocation, I did not see the necessity of going into a decline about it. Besides, I never did value plants or animals that have to be nursed and petted and coaxed to live. If things want to die, I think they'd better die. Provoked by my indifference, one of the tomatoes flared up, and took a new start, put forth leaves, shot out vines, and covered himself with fruit and glory. The chickens picked out the heart of all the tomatoes as soon as they ripened, which was of no conse-quence, however, as they had wasted so much time in the beginning that the autumn frosts came upon them unawares, and there wouldn't have been fruit enough ripe to be of any account, if no chicken had ever broken a shell.

48

49

They appeared aboveground, large-lobed, and vigorous. Large and vigorous appeared the bugs, all gleaming in green and gold, like the wolf in the fold, and stopped up all the stomata and ate up all the parenchyma, till my squash leaves looked as if they had grown for the sole purpose of illustrating net-veined organizations. In consternation I sought again my neighbor the Englishman. He assured me he had 'em on high, too, lots of 'em. This reconciled me to mice. Bugs are not inherently desirable, but a universal bug does not indicate special want of skill in anyone. So I was comforted. But the Englishman said they must be killed. He had killed his. Then I said I would kill mine, too. How should it be done? Oh, put a shingle near the vine at night, and they would crawl upon it to keep dry, and go on early in the morning and kill 'em. But how to kill them? Why, take 'em right between your thumb and finger and crush 'em!

As soon as I could recover breath, I informed him confidentially, that, if the world were one great squash, I wouldn't undertake to save it in that way. He smiled a little, but I think he was not overmuch pleased. I asked him why I couldn't take a bucket of water and dip the shingle in it and drown them. He said, well, I could try it.

I did try it, first wrapping my hand in a cloth to prevent contact with any stray bug. To my amazement, the moment they touched the water they all spread unseen wings and flew away, safe and sound. I should not have been much more surprised to see Halicarnassus soaring over the ridgepole. I had not the slightest idea that they could fly. Of course I gave up the design of drowning them.

I called a council of war. Someone said I must put a newspaper over them and fasten it down at the edges; then the bugs couldn't get in. I timidly suggested that the squashes couldn't get out. Yes, they could, he said— they'd grow right through the paper. Another said I must surround them with round boxes with the bottoms broken out; for, though the bugs could fly, they couldn't steer, and when they flew up they just dropped down anywhere, and as there was on the whole a good deal more land on the outside of the boxes than on the inside, the chances were in favor of their dropping on the outside. Another said that ashes must be sprinkled on them. A fourth said lime was an infallible remedy.

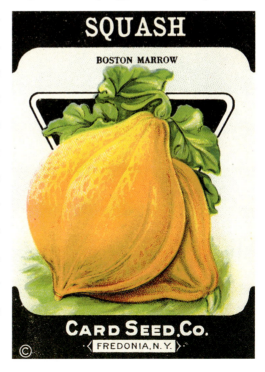

I began with the paper, which I secured with no little difficulty; for the wind—the same wind, strange to say—kept blowing the dirt at me and the paper away from me; but I consoled myself by remembering the numberless rows of squash pies that should crown my labors, and May took heart from Thanksgiving. The next day I peeped under the paper, and the bugs were a solid phalanx. I reported at headquarters, and they asked me if I killed the bugs before I put the paper down. I said no, I supposed it would stifle them; in fact, I did not think anything about it, but if I had thought anything, that was what I thought. I was not pleased to find I had been cultivating the bugs and furnishing them with free lodgings. I went home, and tried all the remedies in succession. I could hardly decide which agreed best with the structure and habits of the bugs, but they throve on all. Then I tried them all at once and all o'er with a mighty uproar.

Presently the bugs went away. I am not sure that they would not have gone just as soon if I had let them alone. After they were gone, the vines scrambled out and put forth some beautiful, deep-golden blossoms. When they fell off, that was the end of them. Not a

squash, not one, not a single squash, not even a pumpkin. They were all false blossoms.

he trees swelled into masses of pink and white fragrance. Nothing could exceed their fluttering loveliness or their luxuriant promise. A few days of fairy beauty, and showers of soft petals floated noiselessly down, covering the earth with delicate snow; but I knew that, though the first blush of beauty was gone, a mighty work was going on in a million little laboratories, and that the real glory was yet to come. I was surprised to observe, one day, that the trees seemed to be turning red. I remarked to Halicarnassus that that was one of nature's processes which I did not remember to have seen noticed in any

botanical treatise. I thought such a change did not occur till autumn. Halicarnassus curved the thumb and forefinger of his right hand into an arch, the ends of which rested on the wrist of his left coat-sleeve. He then lifted the forefinger high and brought it forward. Then he lifted the thumb and brought it up behind the forefinger, and so made them travel up to his elbow. It seemed to require considerable exertion in the thumb and fore-finger, and I watched the progress with interest. Then I asked him what he meant by it.

"That's the way they walk,"
he replied.

"Who walk?"

"The little fellows that
have squatted on our trees."

"What little fellows do you mean?"

"The cankerworms."

"How many are there?"

"About twenty-five decillions, I should think,
as near as I can count."

"Why! what are they for? What good do they do?"

"Oh, no end. Keep the children from eating
green apples and getting sick."

"How do they do that?"

"Eat 'em themselves."

A frightful idea dawned upon me. I believe I turned a kind of ghastly blue.

"Halicarnassus, do you mean to tell me that the cankerworms are eating up our

apples, and that we shan't have any?"

"It looks like that exceedingly."

*T*hat was months ago, and it looks a great deal more like it now. I watched those trees with sadness at my heart. Millions of brown, ugly, villainous worms gnawed, gnawed, gnawed at the poor little tender leaves and buds—held them in foul embrace—polluted their sweetness with hateful breath. I could almost feel the shudder of the trees in that slimy clasp, could almost hear the shrieking and moaning of the young fruit that saw its hope of happy life thus slowly consumed; but I was powerless to save. For weeks that loathsome army preyed upon the unhappy, helpless trees, and then spun loathsomely to the ground, and buried itself in the reluctant, shuddering soil. A few dismal little apples escaped the common fate; but when they rounded into greenness and a suspicion of pulp, a boring worm came and bored them, and they too died.

No apple pies at Thanksgiving. No apple roasting in winter evenings. No pan pie with hot brown bread on Sunday mornings.

They rivaled the appleblooms in snowy profusion, and the branches were covered with tiny balls. The sun mounted warm and high in the heavens, and they blushed under his ardent gaze. I felt an increasing conviction that here there would be no disappointment; but it soon became palpable that another class of depredators had marked our trees for their own. Little brown toes could occasionally be seen peeping from the foliage, and little bare feet left their print on the garden soil. Humanity had evidently deposited its larva in the vicinity. There was a schoolhouse not very far away, and the children used to draw water from an old well in a distant part of the garden. It was surprising to see how thirsty they all became as the cherries ripened. It was as if the village had simultaneously agreed to breakfast on salt fish. Their wooden bucket might have been the urn of the Danaides, judging from the time it took to fill it. The boys were as fleet of foot as young zebras, and presented upon discovery no apology or justification but their heels, which was a wise stroke in them. A troop of rosy-cheeked, bright-eyed little snips in white pantalets, caught in the act, reasoned with in a semicircle, and cajoled with candy, were as sweet as distilled honey, and promised with all their innocent hearts and hands not to do so any more.

Then the cherries were allowed to hang on the trees and ripen. It took them a great while. If they had been as big as hogsheads, I should think the sun might have got through them sooner than he did. They looked ripe long before they were so; and, as they were very plenty, the trees presented a beautiful appearance. I bought a stack of fantastic little baskets from traveling Indian tribes, at a fabulous price, for the sake of fulfilling my long-cherished design of sending fruit to my city friends.

After long waiting, Halicarnassus came in one morning with a tin pail full, and said that they were ripe at last, for they were turning purple and falling off; and he was going to have them gathered at once. He had brought in the first fruits for breakfast. I put them in the best preserve dish, twined it with myrtle, and set it in the center of the table. It looked charming, so ruddy and rural and Arcadian. I wished we could breakfast outdoors; but the summer was one of unusual severity, and it was hardly prudent thus to brave its rigor. We had cup custards at the close of our breakfast that morning, very vulgar, but very delicious. We reached the cherries at the same moment, and swallowed the first one simultaneously. The effect was instantaneous and electric. Halicarnassus puckered his face into a perfect wheel, with his mouth for the hub. I don't know how I looked, but I felt badly enough.

"It was unfortunate that we had custards this morning," I remarked. "They are so sweet that the cherries seem sour by contrast. We shall soon get the sweet taste out of our mouths, however."

"That's so!" said Halicarnassus, who *will* be coarse.

We tried another. He exhibited a similar pantomime, with improvements. My feelings were also the same, intensified. "I am not in luck today," I said, attempting to smile. "I got hold of a sour cherry this time."

"I got hold of a bitter one," said Halicarnassus.

"Mine was a little bitter, too," I added.

"Mine was a little sour, too," said Halicarnassus.

"We shall have to try again," said I.

We did try again.

"Mine was a good deal of both this time," said Halicarnassus. "But we will give them a fair trial."

"Yes," said I, sepulchrally.

We sat there sacrificing ourselves to abstract right for five minutes. Then I leaned back in my chair, and looked at Halicarnassus. He rested his right elbow on the table, and looked at me.

**"Well," said he at last,
"how are cherries and things?"**

"Halicarnassus," said I, solemnly, "it is my firm conviction that farming is not a lucrative occupation. You have no certain assurance of return, either for labor or capital invested. Look at it. The bugs eat up the squashes. The worms eat up the apples. The cucumbers won't grow at all. The peas have got lost. The cherries are bitter as wormwood and sour as you in your worst moods. Everything that is good for anything won't grow, and everything that grows isn't good for anything."

**"My Indian corn, though,"
began Halicarnassus;**

but I snapped him up before he was fairly under way. I had no idea of traveling in that direction. "What am I to do with all those baskets that I bought, I should like to know?" I asked, sharply.

**"What did you buy them for?"
he asked in return.**

"To send cherries to the Hudsons and the Mavericks and Fred Ashley," I replied promptly.

**"Why don't you send 'em, then?
There's plenty of them,
more than we shall want."**

"Because," I answered, "I have not exhausted the pleasures of friendship. Nor do I perceive the benefit that would accrue from turning lifelong friends into lifelong enemies."

"I'll tell you what we can do," said Halicarnassus.
"We can give a party and treat them to cherries.
They'll have to eat 'em out of politeness."

"Halicarnassus," said I, "we should be mobbed. We should fall victims
to the fury of a disappointed and enraged populace."

"At any rate," said he,
"we can offer them to chance visitors."

The suggestion seemed to me a good one—at any rate, the only one that held out any prospect of relief. Thereafter, whenever friends called singly or in squads—if the squads were not large enough to be formidable—we invariably set cherries before them, and with generous hospitality pressed them to partake. The varying phases of emotion which they exhibited were painful to me at first, but I at length came to take a morbid pleasure in noting them. It was a study for a sculptor. By long practice I learned to detect the shadow of each coming change, where a casual observer would see only a serene expanse of placid politeness. I knew just where the radiance, awakened by the luscious, swelling, crimson globes, faded into doubt, settled into certainty, glared into perplexity, fired into rage. I saw the grimace, suppressed as soon as begun, but not less patent to my preternaturally keen eyes. No one deceived me by being suddenly seized with admiration of a view. I knew it was only to relieve his nerves by making faces behind the window curtains.

I grew to take a fiendish delight in watching the conflict, and the fierce desperation which marked its violence. On the one side were the forces of fusion, a reluctant stomach, an unwilling esophagus, a loathing palate; on the other, the stern, unconquerable will. A natural philosopher would have gathered new proofs of the unlimited capacity of the human race to adapt itself to circumstances, from the debris that strewed our premises after each fresh departure. Cherries were chucked under the sofa, into the table drawers, behind the books, under the lamp mats, into the vases, in any and every place where a dexterous hand could dispose of them without detection. Yet their number seemed to suffer no abatement. Like Tityus's liver, they were constantly renewed, though constantly consumed. The small boys seemed to be suffering from a fit of conscience. In vain we closed the blinds and shut ourselves up in the house to give them a fair field. Not a cherry was taken. In vain we went ostentatiously to church all day on Sunday. Not a twig was touched. Finally I dropped all the curtains on that side of the house, and avoided that part of the garden in my walks. The cherries may be hanging there to this day, for aught I know.

But why do I thus linger over the sad recital?

AB UNO DISCE OMNES.

(A quotation from Virgil means, "All of a piece!")

There may have been, there probably was, an abundance of sweet corn, but the broomstick that had marked the spot was lost, and I could in no wise recall either spot or stick. Nor did I ever see or hear of the peas or the beans. If our chickens could be brought to the witness box, they might throw light on the subject.

Yet, sad as my story is, I cannot regret that I came into the country and attempted a garden. It has been fruitful in lessons, if in nothing else. I have seen how every evil has its compensating good. When I am tempted to repine that my squashes did not grow, I reflect that, if they had grown, they would probably have all turned into pumpkins, or if they had stayed squashes, they would have been stolen. When it seems a mysterious providence that kept all my young hopes underground, I reflect how fine an illustration I should otherwise have lost of what Kossuth calls the solidarity of the human race, what Paul alludes to when he says, if one member suffer, all the members suffer with it. I recall with grateful tears the sympathy of my neighbors on the right hand and on the left—expressed not only by words, but by deeds. In my mind's eye, I see again the baskets of apples and pears and tomatoes and strawberries, squash too heavy to lift, and corn sweet as the dews of Hymettus, that bore daily witness of human brotherhood. I remember, too, the victory which I gained over my own depraved nature. I saw my neighbor prosper in everything he undertook. Fertility found in his soil its congenial home, and spanned it with rainbow hues.

Every day I walked by his garden and saw it putting on its strength, its beautiful garments. I had not even the small satisfaction of reflecting that, amid all his splendid success, his life was cold and cheerless, while mine, amid all its failures, was full of warmth—a reflection which, I have often observed, seems to go a great way towards making a person contented with his lot—for he had a lovely wife, promising children, and the whole village for his friends. Yet, not withstanding all these obstacles, I learned to look over his garden wall with sincere joy.

There is one provocation, however, which I cannot yet bear with equanimity. I do hereby beseech all persons who do not wish to have on their hands the burden of my ruined temper, to let me go quietly down into the valley of humiliation and oblivion, and not pester me with the infuriating question,

"How did you get on with your garden?"

am oppressed with a feeling that, whatever welcome my literary venture may meet, I have not, so far as appears in this volume, made a brilliant figure at gardening. I think, therefore, that I ought, in justice to myself, to relate the distinguished success which attended my second attempt. An ordinary person would have been deterred by so unparalleled a series of disasters as befell me from ever making another endeavor; but, for my part, I like always to retire with the honors of war. Therefore, when February crept away to the north, and March came breezing up from the south, I went to a seed shop and laid in an entire new supply of garden ammunition.

I began on a smaller scale than before. My ambition had not forgotten the severe lesson of the past spring. I relinquished the idea of supplying our table with vegetables, and concluded to devote myself solely to the department of the beautiful. Instead of taking the whole estate for a center, and radiating over the land in all directions, I preempted from the waste of corn and potato field a corner, ill-suited, indeed, to my desires and my dreams, but better suited, I was forced to admit, to my inexperience.

70

A square piece of ground, of moderate size, was the basis of my flower bed. The circle described by the drapery of a fashionably-dressed woman, standing in the center, would be scarcely more than contained in it. But does not "Rare Ben" say, "In small proportion we just beauties see, And in small measure life may perfect be"?

It is amazing to note the interest one has in the weather when one becomes a landed proprietor. It is equally amazing to note the coquetry of the weather when it becomes aware of that fact. With the poets, who have hitherto kept me in almanacs, April is a sunny, showery month; May melts into music and warmth; and June is redolent of roses. But, O Messrs. Poets, you have dealt treacherously with me, or else you have studied nature from Chaucer, not from herself.

What did April do for me this year? Blocked me up with a snowstorm. What did May do? Took advantage of her name, entrapped my coal stove into the garret, then benumbed my fingers, and turned me into a Nova Scotian. Nay, Winter, lingering, was not content to chill the lap of May, but even set young June ashivering. The fact is, Spring as a figure of speech, and the prolific mother of figures of speech, is a good thing; but Spring as an institution ought to be abolished. It has outlived its usefulness. It exists only in tradition; and that tradition is productive of much mischief. Our idea of it, derived chiefly from Old English ballads, smells of violets and soft airs, and gay, green woods, and frisking lambs and golden-throated birds. In pursuance of which idea we get up May parties on May Day, and lay aside our flannels, and make ourselves miserable, let alone the rheumatisms and neuralgias and consumptions whose highway we make straight. The blue skies, the greening fields, and the poets aforesaid, conspire to draw us into the trap of raw east wind and chill vapor, from which we return with a stiff neck, a sore throat, and settled melancholy. All this would be obviated if there could only be a general understanding that Winter in this latitude lasts till the Fourth of July, and comes out in spots all summer. We should then know what to depend upon, and the "fair, mild days" would be so many extra blessings thrown in. That is, the rule would be comfortable, and the exceptions delicious; whereas now, the rule is indifferent, and the exceptions intolerable.

Understand, I am not finding fault with the weather, but with our nomenclature. A northeast snowstorm is a splendid thing in its way; only don't let us pretend it is a shower of apple blossoms, and act accordingly.

*B*ut snowy April days and murky May mornings may cultivate the divine virtue of patience, if nothing else, I said to myself, as I stood, flower seeds in hand, awaiting the spring. It came at last, or something which a vivid imagination, combined with the almanac, could call spring, and I leveled and spaded and raked and squared my flower bed that was to be. On the north and south I bounded it with a line of currant bushes; on the east and west with rose bushes. At least, that is what they were given to me for. In my heart I believed they were mere dry sticks, but I stuck them into the ground, nothing wavering. Between the rose sticks I set out pansy roots, and between the currant sticks, dahlias and whatever is the plural of gladiolus.

Next came the question of internal arrange-ment. You may let a forest grow wild. Nature will group her trees, and drape herself with all manner of creeping mosses and trailing berries and sprightly undergrowth, and you shall find nothing amiss. But snip off a little bit of nature, and the case is altered. A garden that you can put in your pocket is nothing if it is not regular. You must have a design, a diagram. I thought of a star. But a star is a great deal easier to think of than it is to make. If you don't believe me, I should just like to have you try it. I have a vague impression that, if I could have got hold of a treatise on geometry, I could have constructed one, but I don't suppose there was such a treatise within twenty miles; so I had to bungle with sticks and strings. However, the result was an obvious star. To be sure, the rays were rather "peaked," and not exactly equidistant at the tips, and somewhat skewy at the center; but it was a very good star for all that. At least, it was more like a star than like anything else. AUT ASTER AUT NULLUS!

When I had completed that, I put outside, between the five rays, two gladiolus roots, a pansy, a circle of candytuft, and one lily of the valley. Then there was nothing to do but wait. That is the beauty of being a farmer. A little provision, a few days of hard work, and the sweet sunshine, the soft rain, the silent dews finish the business. You do not have to hammer away day after day at your lapstone or your sermon. Nature herself puts a shoulder to your wheel, and rolls you on to fortune.

Or would, if it were not for the weeds and chickens and bugs and worms that choke and peck and gnaw her gifts. A few innocent flower seeds will make a remarkable number of enemies; and it is surprising to see how much faster weeds grow than flowers. I wonder what the result would be if one should set out Roman wormwood, and tend it carefully. Would it forget it was a weed, fancy itself a flower, and become shy and sensitive? As it is, I have found it one of the most enterprising of individuals. Before I thought of looking for one of my roots or seeds, up came this Italian bitterness, speedily followed by the pig-plant, close on whose heels tramped the smartweed; and in a twinkling appeared quitch grass and sorrel and a mob of little villainous vines; sprawling things, which had never been planted and never came to anything, and had no business there, and only gave the trouble of pulling them up.

But one warm night something happened. The evening had given no sign; but under the silent moon a host of tiny warriors, clad in Lincoln green, unsheathed their sharp swords, cleft the brown earth, and when the day dawned there they were marshalled in knightly array, along the white lines of my star.

I know few sensations more exquisitely satisfactory than the springing up of something which your own hands have planted. You have, perhaps—if you are a neophyte—had a lurking fear lest you might not detect the difference between the gold and the gilt, have suffered weeds to flourish, lest, in exterminating them, you might ignorantly exterminate something that was not a weed; but when the gold comes, you recognize its gleam. A flower is no more like a weed than if it had never grown. It is pale, and soft, and juicy, and tender. The first lifting of its little face above ground is a mute appeal to your sympathy and protection. It would seem as if a harsh look might crush out its little life. But the weed is a saucy, reckless pushing, defiant, strong-nerved Yankee fellow. "Here I am," he says, tossing his plumes six inches in the air before you knew he was anywhere round. "Here I am. You didn't invite me, but I came, and brought all my brothers, and we are going to have a rollicking time of it. You can give me the cut direct. O yes. But I am not sensitive. I am not overladen with modesty. It is a very nice place, this world, with its sun and dew and rain, and I don't intend to be driven out of it in a hurry."

I suppose every schoolgirl and schoolboy in New England has compared weeds and flowers to the vices and virtues of the human heart; but you don't take in the full force of the illustration till you have a flower bed of your own, and actually see the thing going on with your own eyes. Then you make the illustration yourself, and it seems just as fresh to you as if nobody had ever made it before.

You lay in the brown soil the ugly, shrivelled, insensate seed, but under that unseemly garb the soul of the plant keeps watch and ward. Life is there, hidden in death. When the fulness of time is come, life shall burst its cerements, and mount upward to its fate, which is sunshine and greenness, and royal beauty, and matchless grace.

So this mortal puts on immortality.

79

I suppose a professional gardener might laugh at my flowers. In fact, people do laugh at them who are not professional gardeners for that matter, who are no gardners at all, any more than I am. They think I don't see them, but I do. They think that I think a nasturtium is something very smart, and grand, and recherché. I don't think anything of the sort. I know as well as they that it is a very common, kitchen-gardeny kind of a flower. So are poppies. So are mallows. So are lady's delights, and bachelor's buttons, and pinks, and candytuft, and asters, and coreopsis, and roses; but what of that? Is a thing less beautiful because it is common? The blue sky bends over the evil and the good. The earth unfolds her loveliness to the just and to the unjust. No title deeds can convey possession of the splendor or the beauty of the universe. No landed proprietor can fence in from lowliest eyes the swell of the hills, or the scoop of the valleys. No gas agent can turn off the bland breezes from those who cannot pay monthly bills. No "merchant prince" can adorn his garden with the grandeur and the glory of the sea; while the coarsest clodhopper may cleave its crystal curves, be rocked on its heaving bosom, and sink to rest with its surging lullaby.

God makes his most beautiful things most common, and shall we blame his benevolence, spurning his blessings? A nasturtium "common"—with the heart of a thousand sunsets shrined in its kingly cup, or the shadow of royal robes empurpling its "wine-dark depths"! Common! Shall I see less beauty in its golden gleam because that gleam has flashed brightness into myriads of hearts? Shall it not rather have an added value? The hard hand of labor, the wasted hand of disease, the restless hand of poverty have found peace, and hope, and joy, in training these happy flowers to grasp the sunshine and the glad gifts of the dew. I see on the fields of their scarlet banners the message of goodwill to weary souls. Peering into those glowing caverns, the radiant eyes of little children laugh up to meet my own, and the touch of their tender stems is like the touch of groping baby fingers. Shine on, O fairest messengers of Heaven, and show to all waiting, toiling, disheartened, sorrowful lives

83

A strange and mystic story—
How moistened earthly dust can wear celestial glory.

My horticultural cookbook affirms that nasturtiums make a toothsome salad. I dare say. I should like to see the individual, however, who should venture to go browsing among my nasturtiums. I am strongly opposed to Judge Lynch's code of laws; but I think I should give that person something harder to swallow than the worst salad he ever saw.

A poppy is not like a nasturtium, but it has a fringed, downy beauty all its own. A mystical, crimson languor suffuses the encircling air. Vivid bloodred splashes stain its white softness. Sometimes, in riotous revelling, it hurls back the arrows of the sun, till my dazzled eyes can hardly endure the brightness. But pale or purple, it is enchanted ground. Under that fretted greenery, the poets lie asleep. Hence, far hence, all ye profaner ones! It is not for you to tread the courts of the poppy-crowned god.

> **Amid the bowels of the earth full steepe,**
> **And low, where dawning day doth never peepe,**
> **His dwelling is; there Tethys his wet bed**
> **Doth ever wash, and Cynthia still doth steepe**
> **In silver deaw his ever-drouping hed,**
> **And, more, to lulle him in his slumber soft,**
> **A trickling stream from high rock tumbling downe,**
> **And ever-drizzling raine upon the loft,**
> **Mixt with a murmuring winde, much like the sowne**
> **Of swarming bees, did cast him in a swoone.**
> **.....Careless Quite lyes**
> **Wrapt in eternal silence farre from enimyes.**

So dream the poets. But common people must keep wide awake.

hen my nasturtiums came, they came with a leap. They hardly seemed to have grown. They lifted their broad, shield-shaped leaves one morning, and looked as if they had always been there. But poppies tread delicately. There is just a faint line of green, shading the brown soil. For several days it hardly increases. While you are looking at it, you persuade yourself that nothing will come of it, there is nothing there. But when you are away, you have a very strong impression that something was there, and will "turn up." While you are waiting further developments, the "heated term" comes—dry, dusty, suffocating, blinding, baking, brazen days—when the sun unmasks his batteries, and opens upon you a steady fire. If you want to know how your flowers feel about it, go outdoors barefoot, and the grass that was so tender and cool and dewy in the morning, is curled and crisp, and burns your feet.

85

Presently the parched look of your flower bed excites your compassion. You water it, but the water runs off the hardened surface. You loosen the soil around, and it is a little better. In the height of the drought the spout of the water pot generally comes off, and then your strong plants are drenched with torrents, and for your weak ones you take a colander, which is not "handy." So you blunder on, day after day, wishing and watching for a thundershower or a tin peddler. By and by a cloud in the west appears, rises, spreads, and descends in beautiful and doubly welcome abundance. The dear, benevolent rain! the kindly, saving rain! It is better than a thousand watering pots with the spouts all on. It does the business so easily and so thoroughly. You hardly wonder that

Dannae in a golden tower,
Where no love was, loved a shower.

You are in love with it yourself, and as you stand silent, with smiling eyes, a silver voice begins to well murmurously around you; but just here the rumbling of wheels breaks in upon the murmurous voice, and a tin peddler's cart heaves in sight blossoming with watering pots. Of course you don't buy any, but it is "trying" to see them just then. After this, however, you are in no doubt about the poppies. They leap up into rounded vigor and obviousness, and the whole garden is quickened.

88

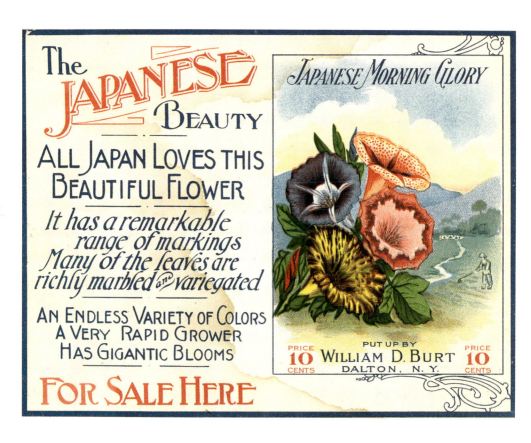

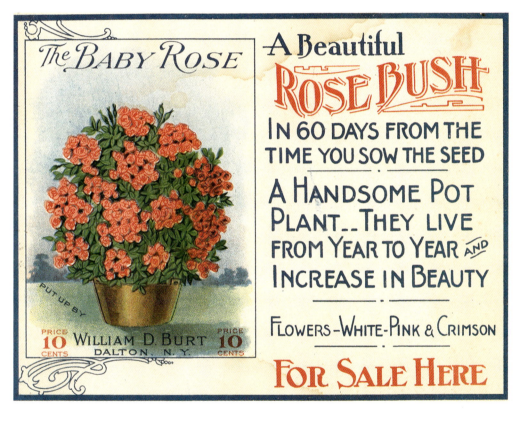

I made a mistake in my planting. I put the seeds in too close, and the center of my star is a perfect tangle. The nasturtiums had the advantage at the start, and they keep it; but they are smothered in their own sweetness, and the gilias and geraniums fairly gasp for breath. A sly little portulaca hides under an overgrown marigold, and cheated me for a long while. I thought several mornings that he had buds on the brink of opening, and sometimes I surely thought I saw buds that had opened and closed again, but that was all, so I set a watch, and one day, just at noon (when I never visited him, and he thought himself safe from intrusion) I spied a flash of solferino, rushed upon him, and caught him in the very act. Since then he has hung out his colors quite openly. My rose sticks have prospered beyond measure. I counted fourteen buds on one of them. My gladiolus is the delight of my eyes,

A daughter of the divinely tall,
And most divinely fair.

I F YOU WANT TO SUCCEED,
— SECURE —
Vick's Floral Guide
FOR 1891.
JAMES VICK, Seedsman, ROCHESTER N. Y.
(OVER.)

y dahlias came up headlong, four or five in a group. Somebody said I must break off all but one. I rejected the vandalism with horror. I am a Republican and a Christian, and I would have no Turks about that could "bear no brother near the throne." It shows the weakness of moral principle that three weeks after, when I saw a bed of dahlias twice as tall as mine, I came home and broke mine off with a bleeding heart. Then they shot up, and a high wind came and twisted and prostrated them remorselessly. Then I hunted up stakes and poles, worn-out broomsticks and dislocated hoe handles, and tied up my dahlias, till my flower bed might have been taken for a returned regiment from a thirty years' war.

Presently one of them "made an effort," and put out a flower, which looked like an agitated turnip. I never saw such a dismal, washed-out rag in my life. I do not think much of dahlias. They are coarse and unsightly in leaf, and forlorn in flower, and ten to one don't flower at all. I call them nothing more than an aristocratic potato.

everal of my most beautiful and promising plants I pulled up,

because Halicarnassus said they were weeds. I did not believe it then,

and the more I think of it, the more I do not believe it still.

It was envy on his part, not weeds on mine.

Still I pulled them up.

So I lost the cream of my garden;

but the skim milk that is left is ravishingly toothsome.

Clay & Richmond, Buffalo, N.Y.

A word to the wise is sufficient

USE THE BAY STATE FERTILIZER,

MANUFACTURED BY

THE CLARK'S COVE GUANO COMPANY,

NEW BEDFORD, MASS

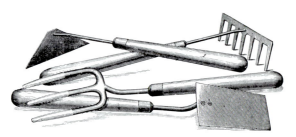

Ladies' and Children's Garden Tools.

Sent by mail, postpaid.

CARROTS.

Fig. 1.   Fig. 2.   Fig. 3.   Fig. 4.